C000018907

THE RAID ON ZEEBRUGGE

THE RAID ON ZEEBRUGGE

-

23rd of April 1918, as seen through the eyes of Captain Alfred Carpenter, VC

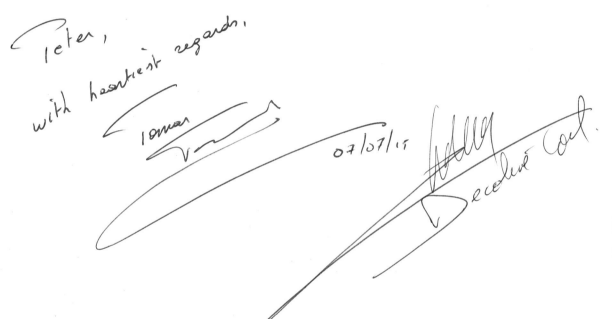

Peter,
with heartiest regards,
Tomas

07/07/15

Decaluwé Carl.

Carl Decaluwé
Tomas Termote

Pen & Sword
MILITARY

The inspiration for the book: a unique collection of glass plates, contained in two wooden boxes,
about the Raid on Zeebrugge. Almost 100 years ago, these were part of the material used by
Captain Carpenter to illustrate the talks he gave about the raid in the years between the wars.

pp. 6-7　　　　　**The monument that commemorates the raid is situated at the foot of the old Mole in Zeebrugge. It was**
　　　　　　　　　inaugurated on 23rd April 1983 and replaces the monument inaugurated in 1925 and subsequently
　　　　　　　　　demolished by the Germans during the Second World War.

FOREWORD

—

In Flanders, we are currently awash with commemorative events, study days, exhibitions dedicated to the Great War and so many new books have been published that it is hard to keep track of them all.

However, what strikes me, when I look at all these various initiatives, is that little - or almost no - attention has been paid to the war at sea, which, of course, was of crucial strategic importance for events on the Western Front.

Two ports on the West Flanders coast (Ostend and Zeebrugge/Bruges) played a vital role in the war. The Germans had effectively converted our coastline into an enormous fortress. The Great War was the first conflict, in which the submarine proved its worth as a serious weapon, and a genuine threat to shipping and seaborne supply routes. Moreover, the German submarine base in Bruges was their first attempt at constructing heavily protected submarine pens. This feat of engineering was to be repeated in many other ports in occupied Europe during World War Two. The Allies frequently attacked both ports, with the aim of putting a stop to German interference with their shipping, but to little avail.

The strategic objective behind the battle of Passchendaele in 1917 was for the allies to seize back the ports of Ostend and Bruges-Zeebrugge, from which the German U-boat fleet had free access to the sea and were able to prey at will on allied shipping.

Despite the enormous sacrifice made by the soldiers in the trenches, the German line proved impossible to break and the allies were therefore forced to find another way of combating the U-boat threat. These plans ultimately crystallized into the Raids and Ostend.

The Raid on Zeebrugge was a bold and daring attempt by the Royal Navy to avoid further losses on the high seas.

This book is a tribute to the British soldiers, sailors and marines who laid down their lives for the freedom of Belgium.

The Belgian people owe an eternal debt of gratitude to Great Britain for what these young men did. In recognition of their sacrifice a bugler still plays The Last Post at the Menin Gate in Ypres every day at exactly 8 pm. On the 9th of July 2015 it will be heard for the 30,000th time.

By sheer chance, Tomas Termote came across a unique collection of photographic plates, which had belonged to Alfred Carpenter, captain of HMS Vindictive - one of the ships that played a key role in the Raid on Zeebrugge. They were used by Carpenter, after the war, to illustrate a series of lectures about the raid. The discovery of these two identical boxes (one of which is now in my own collection) quickly gave us the idea of publishing these incredible photographs in book form. I also sincerely hope that, by 2018, we will have a serious academic study on the Zeebrugge Raid written in the Dutch language. Both the raid and the Great War at sea deserve this attention!

During the Great War, German U-boats sank more than 2,550 allied ships. German losses amounted to 70 U-boats, 145 officers and over 1,000 ratings.

This preface is also dedicated to Captain Charles Fryatt, commander of the merchant ship SS Brussels, who was executed by firing squad.

The execution was carried out in Bruges on 27 July 1916, after the German High Court of West Flanders sentenced him to death for attempting to ram the German submarine U-33 on the open sea.

There are few physical records of the Raid on Zeebrugge, besides the harbour wall (also known as the Mole), the cemetery and two memorials to the fallen. It would be fantastic if we could bring together all the many surviving artefacts, perhaps supplemented by items from other sources, to create an exhibition in honour of all those who lost their lives at sea.

Carl Decaluwé   **Tomas Termote**
Governor of West-Flanders

9

THE RAID ON ZEEBRUGGE

BIOGRAPHY

Captain Alfred Carpenter, VC RN

—

° **17 September 1881**
+ **27 December 1955**

1896: Began his career in the navy, training on HMS Britannia.

1898: Active service as midshipman during the uprising in Crete.

1900: Active service in China during the Boxer Rebellion as sub-lieutenant.

1911: Rescued a sailor who had fallen overboard into the sea from HMS Achilles at Spithead, Portsmouth. For this act of bravery, he was awarded the Bronze Medal by the Royal Humane Society.

1914: At the outbreak of the First World War, he was an administrator on the staff of Sir John Jellicoe.

1915: Navigation officer aboard the battleship HMS Emperor of India.

1917: Promoted to Commander and added to the staff of Admiral Keyes, where he was involved in the planning of the raid on Zeebrugge.

1918: Promoted to the rank of Acting Captain, volunteering to command HMS Vindictive during the raid on Zeebrugge.

1918: During the raid and despite German gunfire and the dark of the night, he was able to manoeuvre HMS Vindictive alongside the Zeebrugge Mole to allow the attack group to disembark.

His cap and binoculars case, both damaged during the raid, are on display at the Imperial War Museum, next to his Victoria Cross. There is a bullet hole in the cap.

1934: Retired from the Royal Navy as Rear Admiral.

1940-1944: Officer-in-charge of the 17th Gloucestershire Battalion of the Home Guard.

1945: Director of shipping at the admiralty.

13

TIMELINE

—

Monday, 22nd of April 1918

10.45 am The assault fleet leaves its anchorage on the Thames.

8.00 pm A rum ration is issued to the crew.

8.45 pm The assault fleet joins up with other ships off the Belgian coast.

9.55 pm The fleet stops so that all non-essential crew members can be taken off the block ships.

10.30 pm The fleet is now 15 miles from Zeebrugge. The landing party are given hot soup.

11.00 pm The raiding party aboard HMS Vindictive are ordered to man
their assault positions, ready for disembarkation.

11.10 pm The towing cables between the block ships are released and
all ships head towards Zeebrugge under their own steam.

11.15 pm The raiding party load their weapons and fix bayonets.

11.35 pm The monitors and destroyers open fire on the shore batteries.

11.40 pm Coastal motor boats and motor launches lay a smoke screen across the coast.

11.56 pm HMS Vindictive emerges from the smoke screen and is only 300 m from the harbour wall.

11.59 pm The German batteries on the harbour wall open fire.

Tuesday, 23rd of April 1918

12.00 midnight HMS Vindictive draws up alongside the harbour wall and
commences disembarkation.

00.05 am The marines and sailors go ashore and a pitched battle with the German defenders ensues.

00.12 am The three block ships slip past the lighthouse undetected and reach the inner harbour.

00.15 am The submarine HMS C3 rams itself between the pilings supporting the viaduct
and the explosives on board are detonated by timefuse.

00.20 am The block ship HMS Thetis is prematurely sunk before reaching
the entrance to the canal.

00.30 am The block ships HMS Intrepid and HMS Iphigenia sail past the now scuttled HMS Thetis.

00.35 am Both remaining block ships are manoeuvred into a sidewise position at the entrance
to the canal and deliberately sunk.

00.40 am The crew of the block ships are taken off by motor launches.

00.50 am Daffodil gives the signal for the landing party to withdraw.

01.05 am Carpenter receives confirmation that the surviving members of the raiding party
are now all safely aboard the Vindictive.

01.10 am Daffodil pulls HMS Vindictive clear of the harbour wall.

03.00 am The assault fleet reaches Dover without any further loss of ships.

15

Captain Alfred Carpenter (4th from left),
with other surviving officers, after the raid.

THE RAID

St. George's Day 1918

—

On the 23rd April 1918, the Royal Navy carried out an attack on German naval installations at the ports of Zeebrugge and Ostend. As this day is the Feast of St. George, patron saint of England, the operation is often referred to as the St. George's Day Raid.

The genesis of this book began with the chance discovery of two wooden boxes in an antiquarian bookshop in Brussels. They were covered in dust and bound together with a leather strap. Inside were a set of photographic plates from the First World War. And not just any old photographs, but photographs of the British raid on Zeebrugge on the 23rd of April 1918. The collection, owned by a family member of one Alfred Carpenter, had come from rural Kent.

The plates were made in the United States in late 1918 and had been used as a visual aid in a series of the Zeebrugge Raid, which Carpenter gave after the war, at the invitation of the Americans and Canadians. He also used them in the early 1920s for a course for naval cadets at Cambridge.

But who was Alfred Carpenter? After a bit of research, it turned out that he was the captain of HMS Vindictive, a British cruiser that played a key role in a night attack on the heavily defended harbour of Zeebrugge. He was one of the 1,700 officers and men aboard 136 Royal Navy ships, which carried out one of the most daring raids of the war: a seaborne attack on what, at the time, was the world's best defended submarine base. Their actions made the small Flemish port of Zeebrugge famous throughout the English-speaking world. The operation was added to the list of battle honours earned by the Royal Marines, while Winston Churchill called the raid "the finest feat of arms of the Great War". The events of that night also led to the highest number of decorations awarded for a single battle in the whole of British military history.

17

18

The Germans built massive submarine pens in the inner harbour at Bruges, known as 'the 8 safe havens'. (TT)

The harbour wall at Zeebrugge, with with protective canopies intended to protect the U-boats from air attacks. (Heiko Hermans)

The German occupation of the Flemish coast

The German advance in 1914 was supposed to follow the Schlieffen Plan, which, among other things, stipulated that the German army should attack through Belgium, in order to seize the French ports of Calais and Dunkirk before pushing south towards Paris. Their intention was to use the ports of Northern France as bases, from which to attack Britain. This was not to be, however. The German army was halted at the first Battle of Ypres in late October 1914 and their advance into France was figuratively and literally bogged down. Calais and Dunkirk remained in French hands and the German navy would now have to use the ports of the coast of Flanders as bases for their attacks on allied shipping.

On the 14th of October 1914, the German naval division occupied Bruges and this part of occupied Flanders came under the overall command of Admiral Ludwig von Schröder. The German admiralty in Berlin was well aware that the Flemish ports of Zeebrugge and Ostend, and especially Bruges, were ideal bases for submarines, destroyers and torpedo boats. Bruges was located 12 km inland and offered these small, but highly effective, vessels complete protection. The canal network of West Flanders gave them access to the coastal ports of Ostend and Zeebrugge, from which they could reach the North Sea and English Channel.

The German navy could not keep its large warships in Ostend or Zeebrugge, due to the inherent risks of crossing the North Sea and because their harbours were too shallow for cruisers or battleships. Yet this was also an advantage, as it gave the German fleet natural protection against attacks from the Royal Navy. The Flemish coast, with its many shallow areas and sandbanks, was, in any case, a nightmare for ships of any depth. All the Germans needed to do now was strengthen and fortify their new base of operations.

From December 1914, the Germans began to convert the Flemish coast into a safe haven and staging post for their smaller vessels, especially U-boats, but also torpedo boats and destroyers. A further advantage was the fact that Flanders was so close to the British coast. From these Flemish ports, U-boats could attack allied ships at will. Thus, the Flemish ports were converted into permanent bases for an entire fleet of U-boats.

U-Flottille Flandern

Although German submarines were already wreaking havoc to allied shipping in the first six months of the war, it was not until March 1915 that Berlin officially designated the U-boats stationed in Flanders as the *Flandern Flottille* (Flanders Flotilla). On the 29th of March 1915, the *Unterseeboots Flottille Flandern* (Flanders Submarine Flotilla) was created under the command of *Korvettenkapitän* Karl Bartenbach. By October 1915, sixteen U-boats had sunk a total of 140 allied ships. Between 1 October 1915 and 30 April 1916, this small fleet managed to sink a further 84 allied ships and 28 ships from neutral countries, with the loss of only two U-boats. In just over a year, the U-boats in the Flandern Flottille had proved highly effective.

In late April 1916, Berlin gave orders for them to stop attacking merchant ships, for fear of provoking the United States, which was still neutral. For the time being, the U-boats largely confined their activities to laying mines in the waters around the mouth of the Thames, the East coast of England and in the approach to the English Channel. From February 1917, U-boat activities were again stepped up and the *Flandern Flottille* had 38 U-boats permanently stationed in Flanders by July of that year.

The Allies were acutely conscious of how dangerous this fleet was to their shipping and carried out air and sea bombardments on Ostend, Bruges and Zeebrugge. The Germans were equally aware of the strategic importance of these craft, which prompted them to build large bunkers and concrete canopies to protect them against air attacks. Between August 1917 and March 1918, a massive submarine base, with 8 concrete pens, was built in the harbour at Bruges, giving the U-boats complete protection.

A UB-I class U-boat enters the harbour at Ostend. (TT)

Allied counter-measures

The Allies did everything possible to combat the U-boat threat. From the very first days of the war, British torpedo boats, cruisers and monitors (shallow-draft vessels used for shore bombardment) regularly shelled the ports of Ostend and Zeebrugge, but with mixed results. Military targets in the ports were hit, but at an unacceptable cost of collateral damage, in terms of civilian lives and property. Moreover, the German submarine fleet was stationed in Bruges, which was 12 km inland and therefore completely immune to bombardment from the sea.

The British also used aircraft. Bombing from the air was more accurate than shelling from the sea and caused much more damage to German installations. Nevertheless, safe inside their concrete pens, the U-boat fleet suffered minimal disruption to its operations.

It was also during this period that the Royal Navy took its first steps towards developing anti-submarine warfare as an integral part of its naval strategy: anti-submarine nets were set up and minefields were laid. The Royal Navy also developed the depth charge and introduced a convoy system. Hundreds of escort ships were deployed to protect Allied shipping against U-boat attack. This measure proved at least a partial success and there was a marked reduction in the tonnage lost between October 1917 and May 1918. However, while these measures certainly succeeded in making life very difficult for the U-boat crews, they were still not enough to stop the U-boat attacks entirely.

The U-boat was clearly a weapon that could not be ignored and those from Flanders were particularly dangerous. In fact, compared to the three largest German bases in Western Europe, they were proportionally the most successful. By the 1st of May 1918, the Flanders fleet had sunk a total of 2,501,000 tons of allied shipping. This amounted to a staggering 600,000 gross registered tons per month, which was the work of a fleet averaging only 22 operational U-boats at any one time.

It became clear that only a direct attack using ground troops could permanently remove the U-boat threat and the Royal Navy was working on concrete plans to do so from as early as the autumn of 1915. Admiral Sir Reginald Bacon, who was in command of the Dover Patrol, wanted to land 9,000 men on the beaches at Ostend using assault craft and capture its harbour at Ostend. These plans were later abandoned, after the Germans strengthened their coastal defences and installed three lines of batteries and defensive emplacements in 1916. In the summer of 1917, the original plans were modified and the Royal Navy opted for a combined operation, involving a land-based assault and an attack from the sea. The main attack would commence close to Ypres in the south, with simultaneous breaches in the German lines at Diksmuide and Nieuwpoort. While these attacks were in progress, the Navy would land three assault boats carrying 14,000 men on the beach between Middelkerke and Westende. The landing never took place because the planned land-based advance from the south proved impossible. It was part of the illfated Passchendaele campaign (the Third Battle of Ypres). On 15 October 1917, all plans for a landing were shelved. From now on, any attack on these targets would have to come from the sea.

Objective Zeebrugge

The Achilles heel of the otherwise impregnable German U-boat base at Bruges was the sea lock at Zeebrugge. All ships, including submarines, going in or out of the port of Bruges had to pass through it. If the sea lock could be destroyed, U-boats would no longer be able to attack shipping from Zeebrugge. In late November 1916, the Royal Navy and Royal Flying Corps made a series of attempts to destroy the lock, but neither naval bombardment nor bombing from the air had any effect. Naval planners then came around to the idea that, if the lock could not be destroyed, it could perhaps be blocked by ramming it with a ship or sinking a ship just in front of the entrance to the lock. The 'sacrificial ship' would have to be able to penetrate the inner harbour, and this would only be possible if the Germans defenders were distracted by a diversionary operation, involving a fleet of smaller ships and a landing troops. In 1918, there were known to be 30 U-boats and 35 torpedo boats in Bruges, which would be rendered useless, if their access to the sea were cut off at Zeebrugge. This was too good an opportunity to pass over.

Yet another victim of the U-boats: a merchant ship sinks after being torpedoed. (TT)

21

The UB-II class U-boat UB-20 using the sea-lock at Zeebrugge. (TT)

The raid was planned by Vice-Admiral Roger Keyes, who was 45 at the time. Keyes had joined the Navy as a cadet in 1885, subsequently serving in India and China, where he blew up an enemy fort single-handedly during the Boxer rebellion. He was later appointed commander of the 8th Submarine Flotilla in Harwich. In 1915, he served in the Mediterranean during the Dardanelles campaign and was given command of the 4th Battle Squadron in 1917. Later in the same year, he took command of the Dover Patrol and thus became responsible for protecting allied shipping in the English Channel. Finding a solution to the U-boat threat was a major part of his task.

Keyes was the ideal man for the job. He was the youngest admiral in the Royal Navy and known as a man of action who was determined to bring the fight to the enemy. He came up with a typically bold plan: a simultaneous attack on Zeebrugge and Ostend that would take the Germans by surprise and allow blockships, filled with concrete, to be scuttled in the entrances to both harbours. The German U-boat fleet would no longer have access to the sea.

22

The full might of the Royal Navy: the Grand Fleet at sea.

Saint George's Day

The attack took place on the night of 22nd-23rd of April 1918 (St. George's Day). 136 ships set off from the mouth of the Thames and headed for the Belgian coast. The main attacking force consisted of 76 ships, which would be directly involved in the raid. The remaining 60 ships, including several monitors armed with heavy guns, were assigned to the task of protecting the flanks of the main force against possible German counter-attacks.

The ships formed three columns. The central column was the main attacking force and included the cruiser HMS Vindictive, which towed the former Mersey ferries HMS Iris and HMS Daffodil behind her. The Vindictive had been given additional armour and a series of fenders, in order to protect her against the impact of hitting the harbour wall. Flamethrowers were also fitted to her upper decks, for use against the German defenders on the wall. She was followed by a minesweeper, 5 motor launches and 5 blockships: HMS Thetis, HMS Intrepid, HMS Iphigenia, HMS Brilliant and HMS Sirius, which were to be scuttled, in order to seal off the entrance to the harbours. The port side column was led by the flagship HMS Warwick, flying Admiral Keyes' flag, followed by 5 destroyers, two of which towed the submarines HMS C1 and HMS C3. The starboard side column consisted of 4 destroyers, an assortment of motor launches and coastal motor boats, which were to lay a smoke screen off the enemy coast at the start of the attack and help evacuate the crews of the blockships, once the latter had been scuttled.

When the Belgian coast came in sight, the motor launches and motor boats took up their position ahead of the main force, in order to lay down the smoke screen. Part of the assault force, including HMS Brilliant and HMS Sirius, now broke away and headed for Ostend, while the main body of the fleet, including the three other blockships, continued on towards Zeebrugge, arriving just before midnight.

When Vindictive, commanded by Captain Carpenter, emerged from the smoke screen, all hell broke loose. She immediately came under heavy German fire, which practically destroyed her upperworks and took out the flamethrowers, yet Carpenter still managed to get Vindictive right up against the harbour wall. The current was so strong at this point that the former Mersey ferries Iris and Daffodil had to push Vindictive against the wall, so that a 250-man storming party, made up of marines and sailors, could scale it using landing ramps, which they had brought with them for that purpose. This would only work if Vindictive was right up against the wall. The storming party had orders to attack the German positions and cause as much destruction as possible to installations, ships and guns – and especially guns that could hit the inner harbour. In reality, the storming party was there to create a diversion, so that the three cement-filled blockships Thetis, Iphigenia and Intrepid could gain access to the inner harbour, where they would be scuttled. As the raiders waited aboard the Vindictive to go ashore, they came under intense fire from the German defenders, which caused a huge number of casualties. To make matters worse, 12 of the 14 landing ramps were severely damaged, so that the storming party had only two serviceable landing ramps that could be used to climb onto the harbour wall. Once in position, they held out under heavy fire for over an hour, in order to convince the Germans that this was the main attack.

A second diversionary operation was the blowing up of a 36-m section of the 'viaduct', a wooden jetty, which linked the harbour wall to the mainland. This was carried out by the British submarine HMS C3, which was carrying 5 tons of explosives in her bow. Lieutenant Sandford and 5 ratings managed to ram the C3 between the lattice work of wooden and iron pilings that supported the viaduct. They set the timer and escaped in one of C3's skiffs. All six were wounded by German small arms fire, but their efforts were rewarded when C3 exploded, thus destroying a large section of the viaduct, cutting off the harbour wall from the shore and making it impossible for the Germans to get reinforcements across to help the embattled defenders.

In the middle of all this confusion, the main operation was in full swing. The three blockships were able to get past the sea wall and into the inner harbour. The plan was to scuttle them just in front of the lock gate. Thetis, under the command of Captain Sneyd, was the lead ship, but its propellers became entangled in one of the steel anti-submarine nets that had been stretched across one section of the harbour.

The submarine HMS C3 was successfully exploded and blew a gap in the 300-m long wood and iron viaduct linking the harbour wall to the shore.

24

*A heavily damaged, but triumphant HMS Vindictive
heads for home on 23 April, after the raid .*

She came to a halt 300 m short of the entrance to the canal and was immediately targeted by the shore batteries. Her crew, many of whom were killed, bravely returned fire. The ship, having been hit repeatedly, was now engulfed in flames and began to sink. As the German guns were now concentrating their shelling on the crippled Thetis, the remaining blockships, Iphigenia and Intrepid, were able to sail on and hardly met with any resistance. Lieutenant Bonham-Carter, captain of the Intrepid, sailed his ship full steam ahead before bringing her hard about, leaving her positioned across the entrance to the canal. He gave orders for the explosives to be detonated and the ship sank where it was. Iphigenia had followed close behind Intrepid, but its commander, Lieutenant Billyard-Leake, initially made a navigational error and headed towards the western section of the harbour wall. He corrected his course and aimed for a free area, east of the now scuttled Intrepid and close to the eastern harbour wall, where he scuttled the Iphigenia. The majority of the crew of the blockships managed to escape in lifeboats and skiffs, before being picked up by two fast motor boats.

About an hour after the attack had begun, HMS Vindictive gave the signal to withdraw. The remaining marines and sailors on the harbour wall fought their way back to the Vindictive. British losses amounted to 214 dead and 383 wounded, with one officer and 15 men taken prisoner, compared to 10 dead and 16 wounded on the German side. Later that same day, Kaiser Wilhelm II visited the battlefield, in order to view the destruction in person.

The attack on Ostend proved a failure. The blockships Sirius and Brilliant missed the entrance to the harbour and ended up to the east of it, on the beach at Bredene, where they came under fire from the shore batteries. The crew were then forced to scuttle both ships.

The war was not over for HMS Vindictive, however. After she had limped into Dover, her superstructure mangled and riddled with holes, she was used as a blockship on 10 May 1918, in a second attempt to block the Ostend harbour entrance. Sadly, this too was unsuccessful. The Vindictive, skippered this time by Commander Alfred Godsal, was supposed to manoeuvre into a broadside position, blocking the access channel, but in the end had to be scuttled close to the eastern side of the harbour wall, which only partially blocked the entrance to the canal.

A moral victory

The attack on Zeebrugge was an enormous achievement for the Royal Navy, but in practical terms the blockships did little to stop U-boats going in and out of the harbour. On the 25th of April, just two days after the raid, UB-16 became the first German submarine to slip past the wrecks at high tide and into the open sea. A few weeks later, the Germans removed part of the harbour wall on the west bank of the canal and dredged the area around the blockships. Medium-sized and even large submarines could again use the canal as before.

For Britain, the Saint George's Day Raid thus remained a moral victory rather than a military success. The operation demonstrated that the German U-boat bases were not invulnerable. By successfully attacking the Flemish coast, Keyes had restored confidence in the Royal Navy and bolstered the belief that the Allies could still win the war. A record number of medals were awarded for the raid, especially considering that the entire operation was of much shorter duration and far less costly in terms of casualties than an average infantry assault on the Western Front. Most controversial of all, the decorations awarded included 11 Victoria Crosses. Since its introduction in 1856, during the Crimean war, the VC has only been awarded 1,356 times and always for examples of truly exceptional bravery or sacrifice. Since the Second World War, only 16 VCs have been awarded. Alfred Carpenter was among those who received the Victoria Cross, which reflected his pivotal role in the events of that night.

25

Wounded, but in good spirits, marines and sailors pose for the camera.

The raid seen through Carpenter's eyes

Alfred Francis Blakeney Carpenter was born into a naval family in Barnes, Surrey in 1881. After joining the Royal Navy as a cadet in 1897, he first served in Crete during the 1898 uprising and later in China during the Boxer Rebellion, as part of the naval brigade dispatched to Kiautschou to restore order. He was promoted to Sub-Lieutenant in 1903, before specializing in navigation and achieving the rank of full Lieutenant in 1911. When war broke out in 1914, he joined the staff of Admiral Sir John Jellicoe, on HMS Iron Duke. In 1915, he became navigating officer on HMS Emperor of India. By 1917, he had gained sufficient experience to secure a post on the staff of Vice-Admiral Roger Keyes, who had recently been appointed Director of Planning at the Admiralty, and was therefore involved in the secret planning of the attacks on Zeebrugge and Ostend. Keyes wrote in his memoirs: "Commander Carpenter's gift for going into the minutest details with the most meticulous care, greatly assisted me in preparing a detailed plan and orders, which embodied the work of several officers". This was high praise indeed.

Clearly, Keyes regarded Carpenter as an exceptional officer. He had a detailed knowledge of all aspects of the operation, which he had helped to plan, and also understood that the attack on Zeebrugge was to be conducted in the aggressive spirit that characterizes the best traditions of the Royal Navy. It comes as no surprise, therefore, that Keyes chose Carpenter to command the Vindictive.

Carpenter was promoted to the rank of Captain for the operation, but his duties were limited to command of the ship itself. Command of the storming party, which was to scale the harbour wall, was assigned to Captain Halahan, who outranked Carpenter. It took a combined force of marines and sailors to create a diversion, in order to draw the attention of the German defenders away from the main thrust of the operation, so that the blockships could penetrate the inner harbour and reach the sea lock, which gave access to the Bruges ship canal. It fell to Carpenter to manoeuvre the Vindictive into position against the harbour wall, which was crucial to the success of the attack. In the end, Carpenter brought the ship to a halt at 340 m from the intended point of disembarkation, so that the marines and sailors in the raiding party went ashore at a considerable distance from the shore guns that they were supposed to take out. It was typical of Carpenter that he acknowledged his mistake, explaining that the smoke screen and explosions made it almost impossible to make out any recognisable features on the harbour wall. Nevertheless, Keyes had nothing but praise for the calm manner, in which Carpenter conducted himself, his skill in navigating without incident through heavily mined waters in complete darkness and how he was able to bring the Vindictive against the harbour wall, while under heavy and constant fire. His bravery set an example to his men and their combined actions ensured that the mission was successful. The fact that he was able to get his heavily damaged ship away from the harbour wall and safely back to Dover after the attack was further testimony to his seamanship.

Keyes asked Carpenter, as the highest ranking surviving officer, to recommend men for medals, but he refused, arguing that he could not single out a few individuals when everyone involved had done his absolute best. He also refused to take part in the ballots held, in which each ship that had taken part in the raid nominated one officer and one candidate from the ranks to receive a medal. The ballot went ahead nonetheless. Among other medals, including the DSO and DSC, 8 Victoria Crosses were awarded to men who had taken part in the raid and whose valour was beyond any doubt. One of these men was Carpenter. His promotion to captain was made permanent. He was also honoured by France, receiving the *Croix de Guerre* with Palm and being made a *Chevalier* of the *Légion d'honneur*. In 1921, he wrote a very detailed description of the attack entitled "The Blocking of Zeebrugge".

After the raid, in 1918 and 1919, he undertook a lecture tour of the United States/Canada and later taught a course for Naval officers at Cambridge. In the 1920s, he commanded various Royal Navy ships. He rose to the rank of vice-admiral and retired in 1934. He died at his home "Chantersluer" in St. Briavels, Gloucestershire, in 1955.

Traces of memory

While it is, of course, well-remembered in Britain, the Raid on Zeebrugge has not been forgotten in Belgium either. Several street names in Zeebrugge recall the events of St George's Day 1918, such as 'Blockship street' and 'Admiral Keyes Square'. A monument now stands at what was once the base of the harbour wall, which commemorates the raid, whilst the bow of HMS Vindictive recently moved to its new home on the eastern pier in Ostend.

King George V, King Albert of Belgium, General Haig and Captain Carpenter visit the harbour wall at Zeebrugge after the war. The visit was staged and probably refers to a different location, because the iconic lighthouse was later refurbished there.

23RD OF APRIL 1918, AS SEEN THROUGH
THE EYES OF CAPTAIN ALFRED CARPENTER, VC

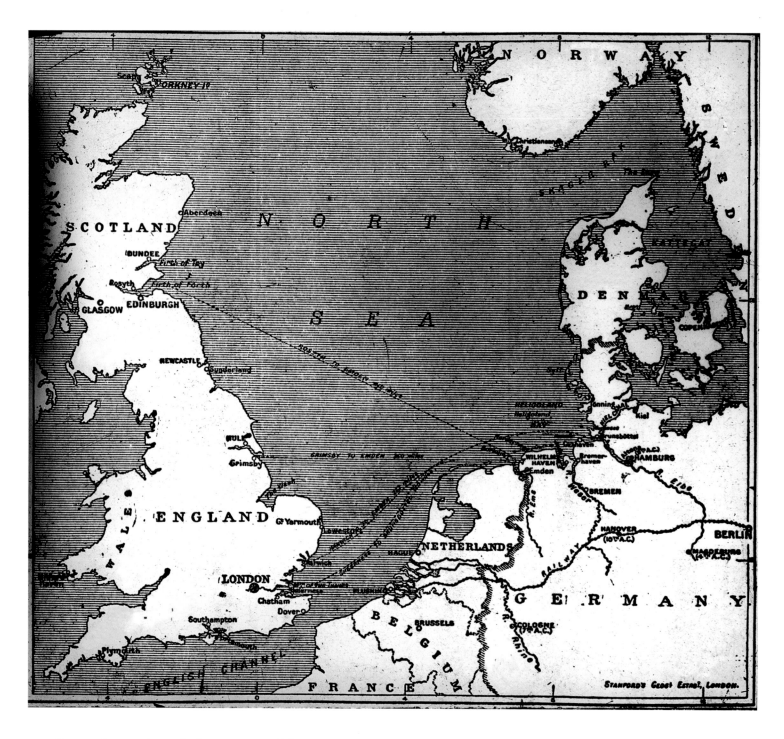

*Distances between the north German ports and the Royal Navy's
principal bases at Rosyth, Grimsby, Harwich and Sheerness.*

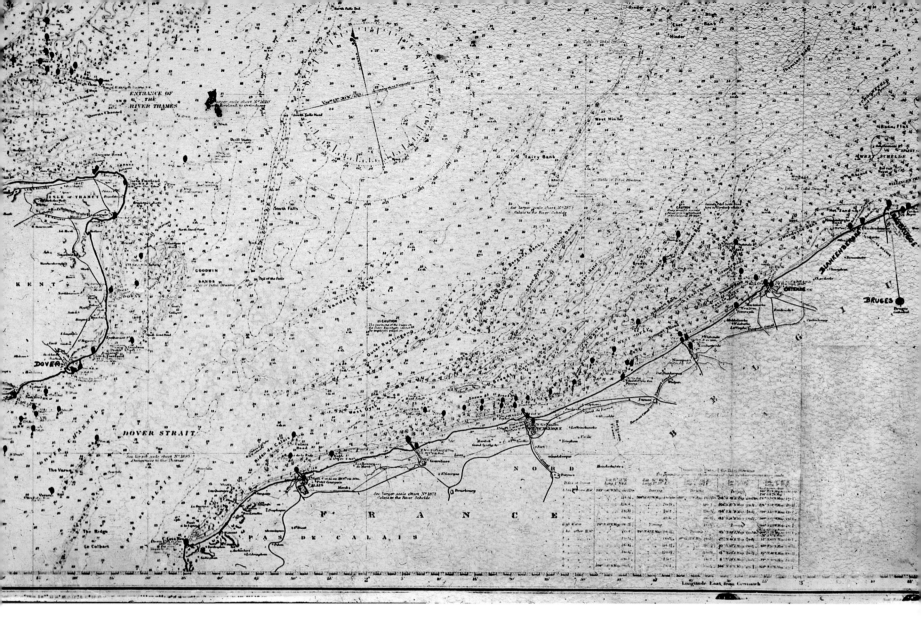

*Map of the Flemish Banks, showing how close the German-occupied
ports of Zeebrugge and Ostend were to the Thames estuary and the Channel.*

32

The full might of the Royal Navy: the Grand Fleet at sea.

A British Destroyer stands guard over a large
oil slick where a U-boat has just been sunk.

King George V.

A pre-war view of the 2.5 km long seawall at Zeebrugge.

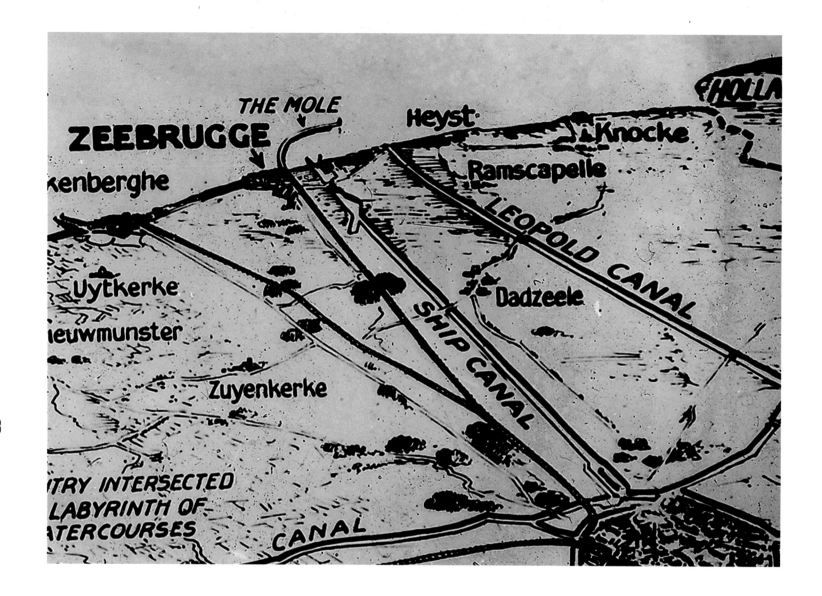

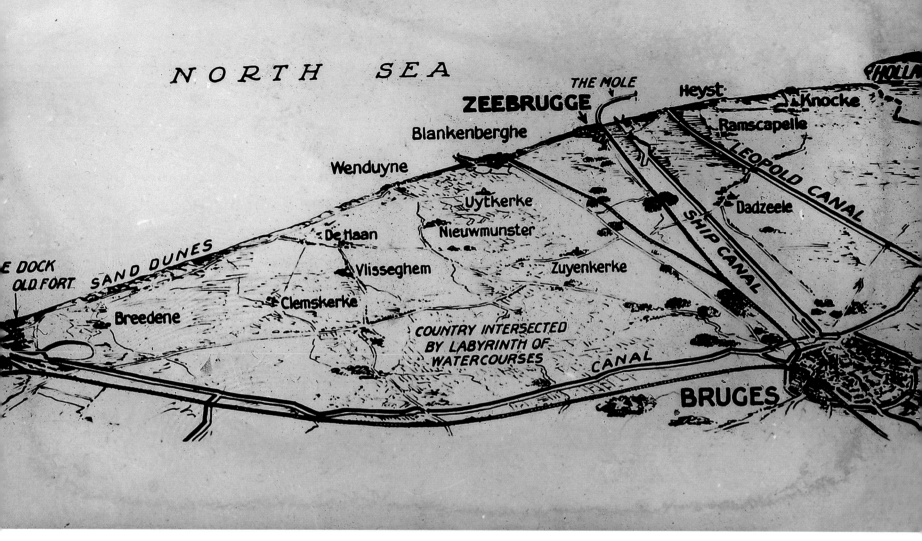

NORTH SEA

THE MOLE

ZEEBRUGGE

Blankenberghe

Heyst

Knocke

Ramscapelle

Wenduyne

LEOPOLD CANAL

Uytkerke

Dadzeele

Nieuwmunster

SHIP CANAL

De Haan

SAND DUNES

Vlisseghem

Zuyenkerke

E DOCK
OLD FORT

Clemskerke

COUNTRY INTERSECTED
BY LABYRINTH OF
WATERCOURSES

Breedene

CANAL

BRUGES

HOLLA

The Flemish coast and the ports to be blocked: Zeebrugge and Ostend.

HMS Vindictive, an Arrogant class cruiser built in 1898, shortly before joining the fleet.

Two former Mersey ferries, Daffodil and Iris, were to play a crucial role in the raid: assisting HMS Vindictive.

*Daffodil had to push HMS Vindictive
to hold her in place against the harbour wall.*

Iris got into difficulties and most of the marines and sailors aboard her were unable to get onto the seawall.

Small boats, such as these motor launches,
would play a vital supporting role during the raid.

The submarine HMS C3, towed by HMS Trident.

*In addition to motor launches, fast coastal motor boats (CMBs)
were used to get the crews off the blockships once they were in position.*

48

*A smokescreen was laid along the entire enemy coast
in order to provide cover for the assault fleet.*

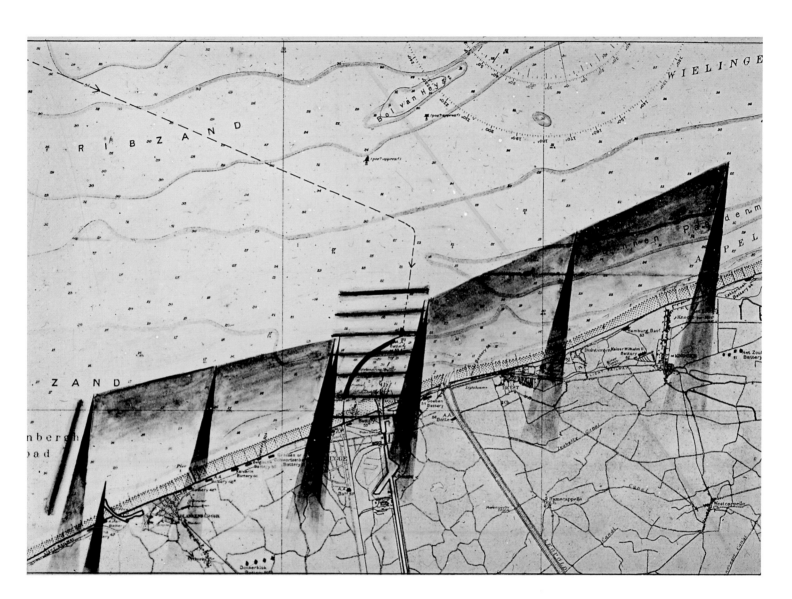

Map showing the section of coastline to be covered by the smokescreen.

It was feared that the German defenders might use gas shells.
Royal Navy gunners demonstrate the use of gas masks.

HMS Vindictive just before sailingon the 22nd of April.
Her upper works have been reinforced to offer maximum protection.

Fourteen wooden landing ramps were fixed to the port side of HMS Vindictive
so that the marines and sailors could storm the harbour wall.

HMS Vindictive sails for Zeebrugge in the late afternoon of the 22nd of April 1918.

ENTRANCE CHANNEL

The raiders' key objective: the sea wall and inner harbour at Zeebrugge.

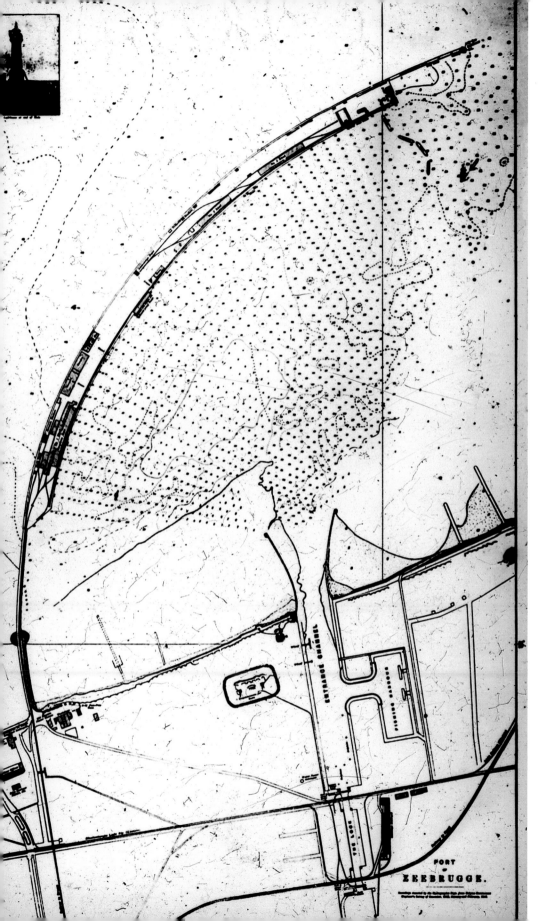

PORT
ZEEBRUGGE.

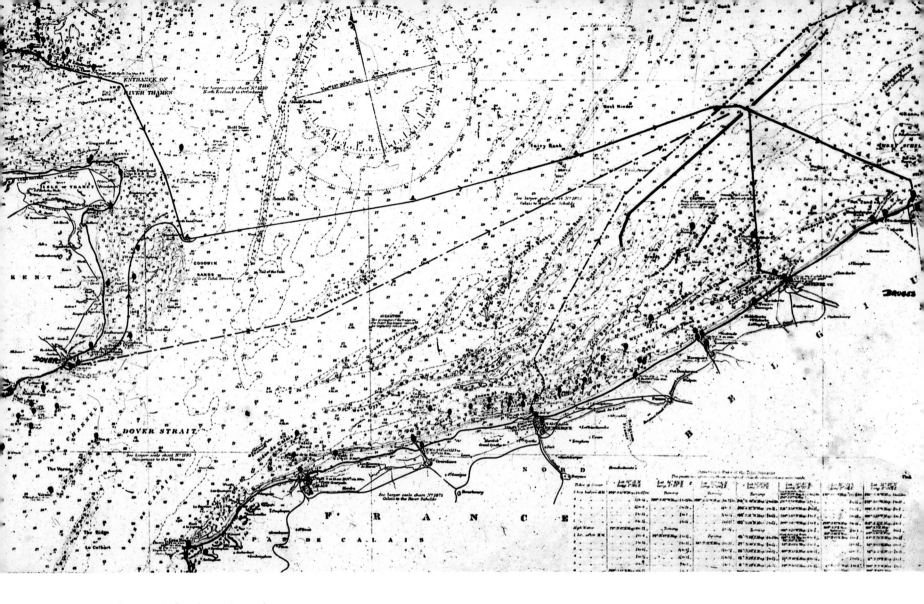

The assault fleet leaves its anchorage
in the Thames and heads for the Flemish coast.

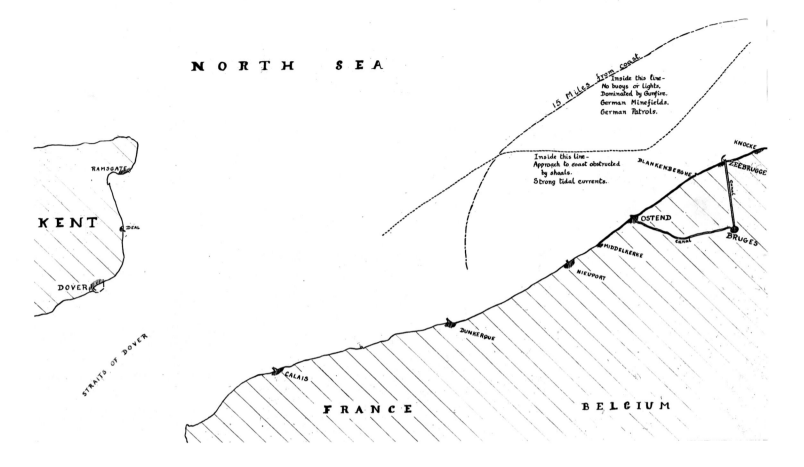

The obstacles facing the raiders: coastal batteries, minefields,
enemy patrol boats, sandbanks, shallow waters and strong currents.

The components of the assault fleet and their respective objectives.

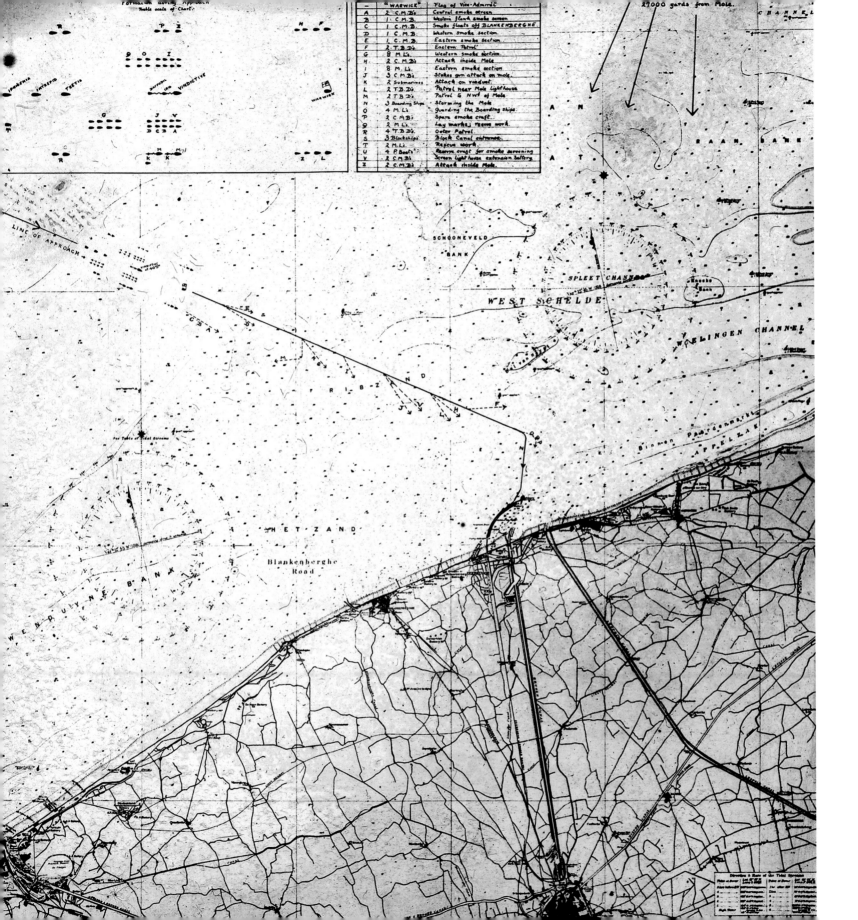

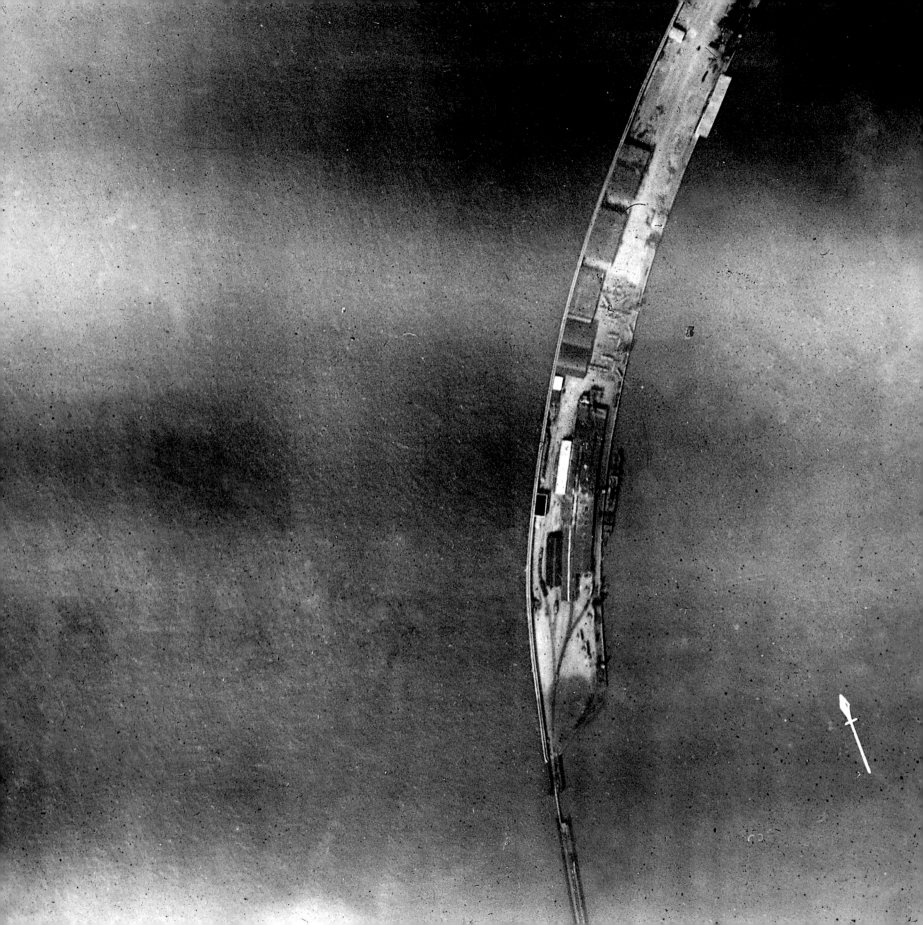

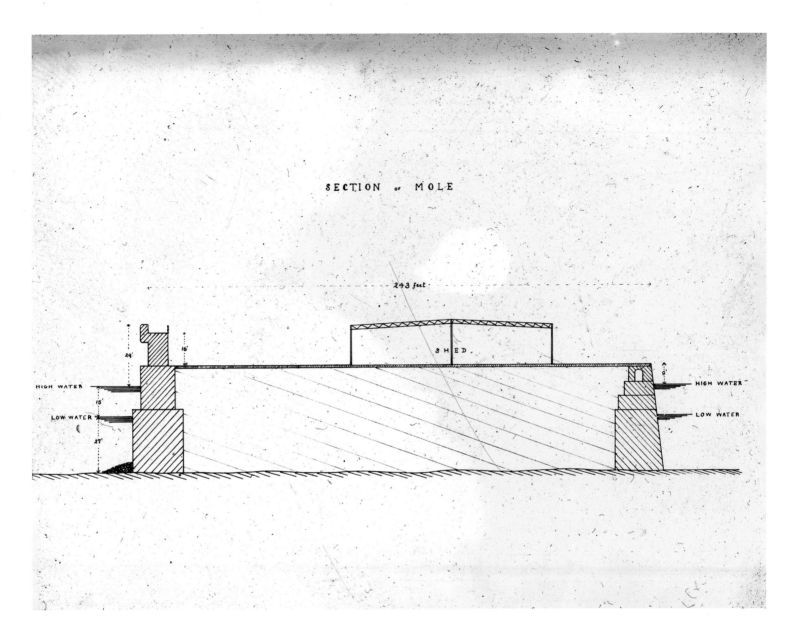

SECTION of MOLE

243 feet

SHED

HIGH WATER

LOW WATER

HIGH WATER

LOW WATER

Cross-section of the heavily fortified harbour wall, showing the huge difference in water level between high and low tides.

The harbour wall at Zeebrugge: HMS Vindictive's objective.

The key objective of the raid:
blocking the entrance to the canal in the direction of Bruges.

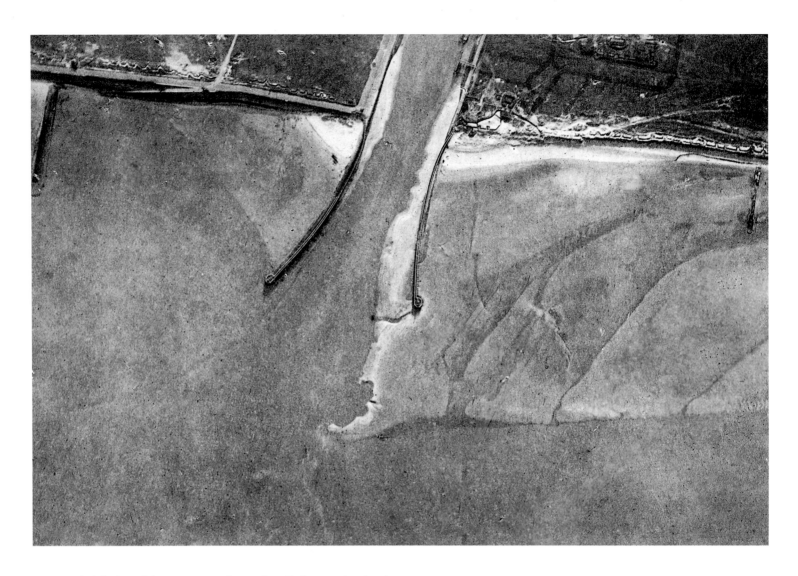

Aerial view of the entrance to the canal at Zeebrugge, showing the gap between the two harbour walls, where the blockships had to be scuttled.

The base of the harbour wall and the 300-m long wood and iron viaduct which the submarine HMS C3 had to destroy.

HMS Vindictive was required to moor itself against the sea-facing side of the harbour wall so as to provide a diversion that would give the blockships time to penetrate the inner harbour.

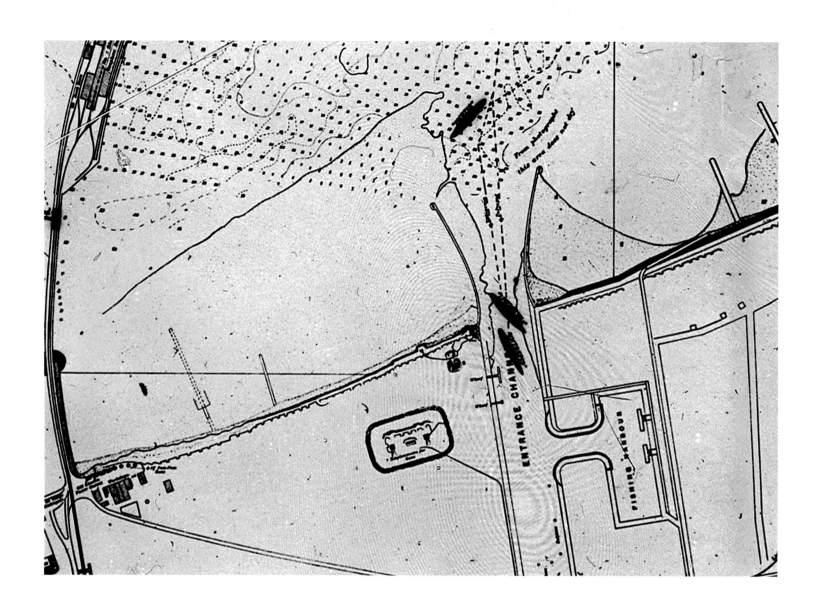

General view of the harbour at Zeebrugge, showing the location of HMS Vindictive, Daffodil and Iris on the sea-facing side of the wall and the three blockships in the entrance to the canal.

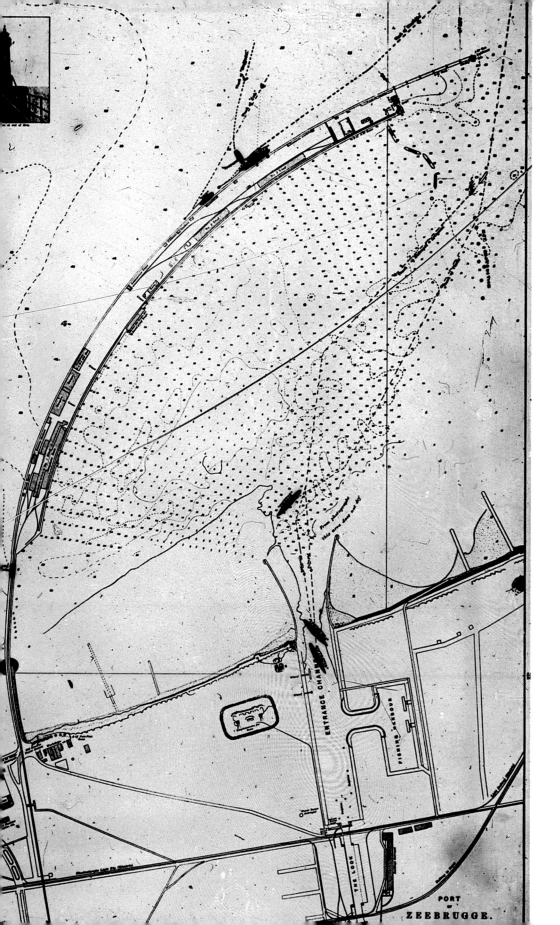

PORT
OF
ZEEBRUGGE.

73

This photograph, taken after the raid, shows the fenders fitted to the port side of HMS Vindictive as protection against the impact of hitting the harbour wall.

At around midnight HMS Vindictive drew herself up against the harbour wall so that the marines and sailors could disembark.

During the attack, SS Brussels, which lay at anchor alongside the seawall, was torpedoed and sunk. This British merchant ship had been captured at sea earlier in the war by German torpedo boats and served in Zeebrugge as an accommodation ship. The photo shows the foremast and 2 funnels sticking out above the surface of the inner harbour.

The landing party's objective was to take out the 8.8 and 10.5 cm guns at the end of the seawall.

Charles John de Lacy (1856–1929) was one of the best-known British naval artists of his time. He painted HMS Vindictive during the attack, as well as various battle scenes on the Mole, which he was able to picture from the stories told to him by Captain Carpenter.

The marines and sailors storm the harbour wall.

Lighthouse at
end of Mole

Tackle for raising the 'brows'

Stern of 'VINDICTIVE'

Ventilators
riddled with
shell splinters

ally built
r deck →

Bridge of
'VINDICTIVE'

12 out of the 14 specially-constructed landing ramps
were rendered useless by German artillery fire.

German shore batteries lay down a murderous barrage of fire,
causing huge numbers of casualties during the first wave of the attack.

The positions of HMS Vindictive,
Daffodil and Iris against the harbour wall.

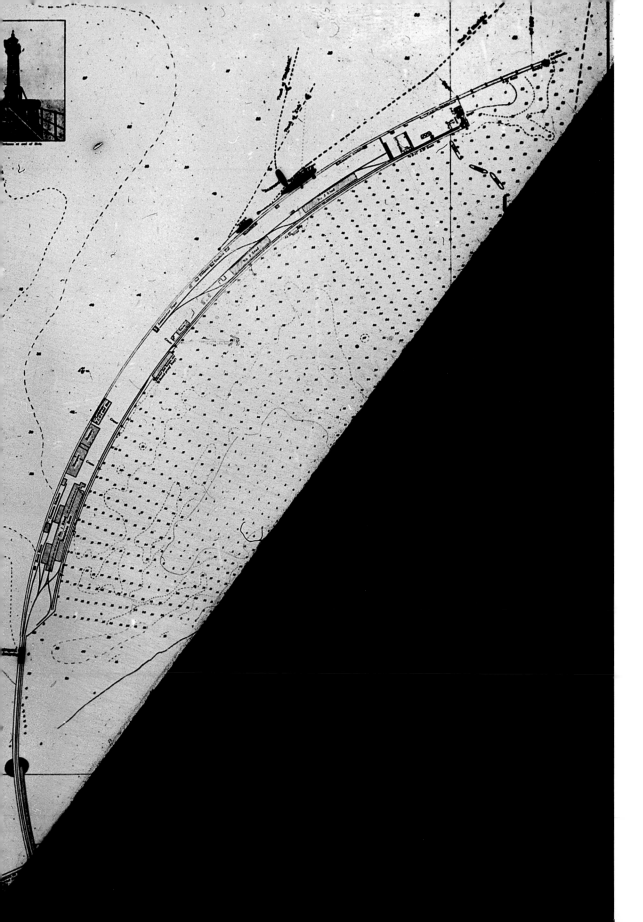

The upper works of the assault ships stuck out above the top of the seawall and came under constant fire.

HMS Vindictive's funnels showing the extreme damage caused by enemy fire.

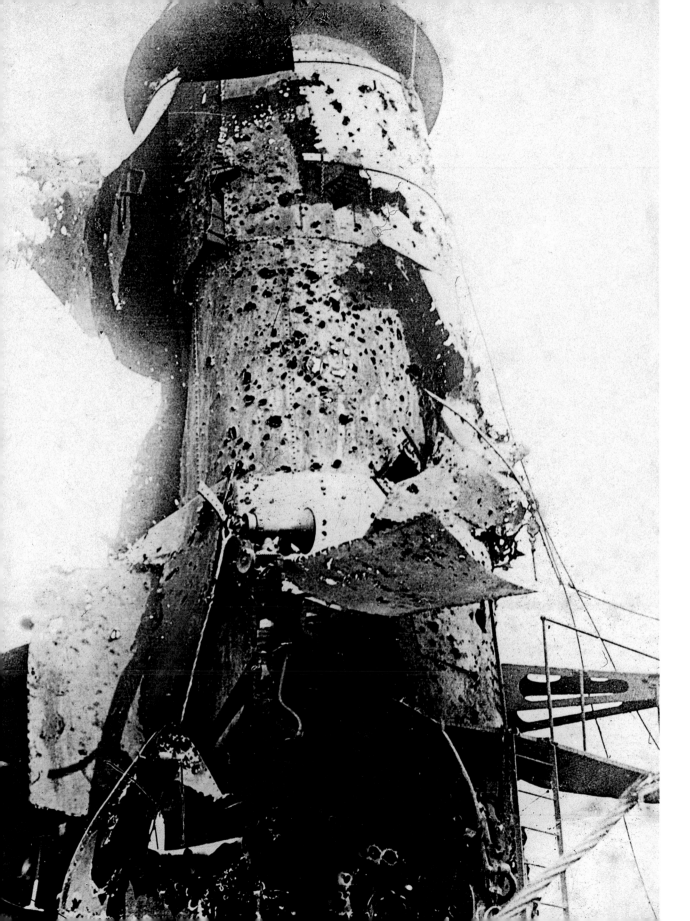

*General view of the harbour side of the seawall, showing
fighting between the raiding party and the German defenders.*

HMS Vindictive's heavily damaged bridge and fore mast.

89

The upper works of the ageing cruiser
seem to have drawn all the German fire.

*The bow of HMS Vindictive, protected with numerous mattresses
and fitted with an armour-plated flame-thrower hut on her port side.*

All the gunners on the assault vessels were given gasmasks in case the defenders fired gas shells.

Explosives in the bow of HMS C3 were succesfully detonated and exploded a gap in the 300-m long wood and iron viaduct linking the harbour wall to the shore.

Wounded, but in good spirits, marines and sailors pose for the camera.

Captain Alfred Carpenter (4th from left),
with other surviving officers, after the raid.

*The heaviest fire that the blockships had to endure came
from shore batteries on either side of the entrance to the canal.*

**The blockship HMS Thetis was scuttled a few
hundred metres short of the entrance to the canal.**

The scuttled blockships HMS Intrepid and HMS Iphigenia partially blocking the entrance to the sea lock.

The scuttled blockships HMS Intrepid, HMS Iphigenia and HMS Thetis partially blocking the entrance to the sea lock.

The scuttled blockships HMS Intrepid and HMS Iphigenia partially blocking the entrance to the sea lock.

A German officer inspects the wrecks of the blockships at high tide.

A heavily damaged, but triumphant HMS Vindictive
heads for home on the 23rd of April, after the raid.

HMS Vindictive in Dover on the 24th of April, one day after the raid.

HMS Vindictive in Dover harbour on the 24th of April, after the raid.

*An aerial photograph showing that the entrance
to the canal had been partially blocked.*

© Eurosense

The port of Zeebrugge in 2015. The harbour has seen extensive expansion during the 1980's and and little remains of the original situation prior to WWI, the shape of the Mole and the entrance to the sea channel remain relatively unchanged.

Detail from the altimeter of the aircraft from which the photo was taken.

The blockships at high tide.

The wrecks at low tide.

Photograph of the entrance to the
sea canal at Zeebrugge as it is today.

Here lie
Three British officers
Seven British marines
Two British sailors
Two British stokers

Sleep now, albeit in a distant grave, deeply mourned,
the love in our hearts will live on.

War grave containing the remains of 14 British dead burried
by the Germans near the St. Donaas church in Zeebrugge.

HIER RUHEN

DREI ENGL. OFFIZIERE
SIEB. ENGL. SEESOLDAT
ZWEI ENGL. MATROSEN
ZWEI ENGL. HEIZER

Nun schlaf denn
wohl im fernen Grab
beweint im tiefen
Schmerz, die Liebe,
die dich hier umgab,
lebt fort in unserem
Herz.

The surviving members of the crew of HMS Vindictive wave triumphantly to the camera after reaching Dover.

King George V greets one of the sailors who took part in the raid on Zeebrugge.

120

King George V, King Albert of Belgium, General Haig, Captain Carpenter and other high ranking military personel visit the harbour wall at Zeebrugge after the war. The visit was staged and probably refers to a different location, because the iconic lighthouse was added to the photograph.

*Admiral Beatty, commander of the Grand Fleet, in conversation
with senior Italian and American naval officers.*

Rule Britannia!

The Victoria Cross, Great Britain's highest military medal, is awarded "For Valour". In total, 8 VCs were awarded for the attack on Zeebrugge and 3 for Ostend.

INDEX

pp. 30 – Distances between the north German ports and the Royal Navy's principal bases at Rosyth, Grimsby, Harwich & Sheerness.

pp. 35 – King George V.

pp. 41 – Two former Mersey ferries, Daffodil and Iris, were to play a crucial role in the raid: assisting HMS Vindictive.

pp. 45 – Small boats, such as these motor launches, would play a vital supporting role during the raid.

pp. 31 – Map of the Flemish Banks showing how close the German-occupied ports of Zeebrugge and Ostend were to the Thames estuary and the Channel.

pp. 37 – A pre-war view of the 2.5 km long seawall at Zeebrugge.

pp. 42 – Daffodil had to push HMS Vindictive to hold her in place against the harbour wall.

pp. 47 – In addition to motor launches, fast coastal motor boats (CMBs) were used to get the crews off the blockships once they were in position.

pp. 32 – The full might of the Royal Navy: the Grand Fleet at sea.

pp. 38 – The Flemish coast and the ports to be blocked: Zeebrugge and Ostend.

pp. 43 – Iris got into difficulties and most of the marines and sailors aboard her were unable to get onto the seawall.

pp. 48 – A smokescreen was laid along the entire enemy coast in order to provide cover for the assault fleet.

pp. 33 – A British Destroyer stands guard over a large oil slick where a U-boat has just been sunk.

pp. 40 – HMS Vindictive, an Arrogant class cruiser built in 1898, shortly before joining the fleet.

pp. 44 – The submarine HMS C3, towed by HMS Trident.

pp. 49 – Map showing the section of coastline to be covered by the smokescreen

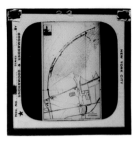

pp. 50 - It was feared that the German defenders might use gas shells. Royal Navy gunners demonstrate the use of gas masks.

pp. 57 - The raiders' key objective: the sea wall and inner harbour at Zeebrugge

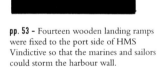

pp. 52 - HMS Vindictive just before sailing on the 22nd of April. Her upper works have been reinforced to offer maximum protection.

pp. 58 - The assault fleet leaves its anchorage in the Thames and heads for the Flemish coast.

pp. 62 - The harbour wall at Zeebrugge: HMS Vindictive's objective.

pp. 53 - Fourteen wooden landing ramps were fixed to the port side of HMS Vindictive so that the marines and sailors could storm the harbour wall.

pp. 59 - The obstacles facing the raiders: coastal batteries, minefields, enemy patrol boats, sand-banks, shallow waters and strong currents.

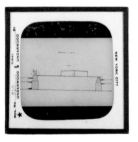

pp. 63 - Cross-section of the heavily fortified harbour wall, showing the huge difference in water level between high and low tides.

pp. 66 - Aerial view of the entrance to the canal at Zeebrugge, showing the gap between the two harbour walls, where the blockships had to be scuttled.

pp. 54 - HMS Vindictive sails for Zeebrugge in the late afternoon of the 22nd of April 1918.

pp. 61 - The components of the assault fleet and their respective objectives.

pp. 65 - The key objective of the raid: blocking the entrance to the canal in the direction of Bruges.

pp. 67 - The base of the harbour wall and the 300-m long wood and iron viaduct which the submarine HMS C3 had to destroy.

pp. 69 - HMS Vindictive was required to moor itself against the sea-facing side of the harbour wall so as to provide a diversion that would give the blockships time to penetrate the inner harbour.

pp. 74 - The landing party's objective was to take out the 8.8 and 10.5 cm guns at the end of the seawall.

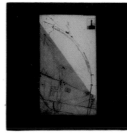

pp. 81 - The positions of HMS Vindictive, Daffodil and Iris against the harbour wall.

pp. 84 - HMS Vindictive's funnels showing the extreme damage cause by enemy fire.

pp. 71 - General view of the harbour at Zeebrugge, showing the location of HMS Vindictive, Daffodil and Iris on the sea-facing side of the wall and the three blockships in the entrance to the canal.

pp. 77 - The marines and sailors storm the harbour wall.

pp. 82 - The upper works of the assault ships stuck out above the top of the seawall and came under constant fire.

pp. 85 - HMS Vindictive's funnels showing the extreme damage cause by enemy fire.

131

pp. 72 - At around midnight HMS Vindictive drew herself up against the harbour wall so that the marines and sailors could disembark.

pp. 78 - German shore batteries lay down a murderous barrage of fire, causing huge numbers of casualties during the first wave of the attack.

pp. 73 - This photograph, taken after the raid, shows the fenders fitted to the port side of HMS Vindictive as protection against the impact of hitting the harbour wall.

pp. 79 - 12 out of the 14 specially-constructed landing ramps were rendered useless by German artillery fire.

pp. 87 - General view of the harbour side of the seawall, showing fighting between the raiding party and the German defenders.

pp. 89 - HMS Vindictive's heavily damaged bridge and fore mast.

pp. 95 - Explosives in the bow of HMS C3 were succesfully detonated and exploded a gap in the 300-m long wood and iron viaduct linking the harbour wall to the shore.

pp. 99 - The heaviest fire that the blockships had to endure came from shore batteries on either side of the entrance to the canal.

pp. 104 - A German officer inspects the wrecks of the blockships at high tide.

pp. 90 - The upper works of the ageing cruiser seem to have drawn all the German fire.

pp. 96 - Wounded, but in good spirits, marines and sailors pose for the camera.

pp. 101 - The scuttled blockships HMS Intrepid and HMS Iphigenia partially blocking the entrance to the sea lock.

pp. 106 - A heavily damaged, but triumphant HMS Vindictive heads for home on the 23rd of April, after the raid.

pp. 92 - The bow of HMS Vindictive, protected with numerous mattresses and fitted with an armour-plated flame-thrower hut on her port side.

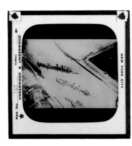

pp. 97 - Captain Alfred Carpenter (4th from left), with other surviving officers, after the raid.

pp. 102 - The scuttled blockships HMS Intrepid, HMS Iphigenia and HMS Thetis partially blocking the entrance to the sea lock.

pp. 107 - HMS Vindictive in Dover on the 24th of April, one day after the raid.

pp. 93 - All the gunners on the assault vessels were given gas masks in case the defenders fired gas shells.

pp. 89 - The blockship HMS Thetis was scuttled a few hundred metres short of the entrance to the canal.

pp. 103 - The scuttled blockships HMS Intrepid and HMS Iphigenia partially blocking the entrance to the sea lock.

pp. 109 - HMS Vindictive in Dover harbour on the 24th of April, after the raid.

pp. 119 – King George V greets one of the sailors who took part in the raid on Zeebrugge.

pp. 118 – The surviving members of the crew of HMS Vindictive wave triumphantly to the camera after reaching Dover.

pp. 121 – King George V, King Albert of Belgium, General Haig, Captain Carpenter and other high ranking military personel visit the harbour wall at Zeebrugge after the war.

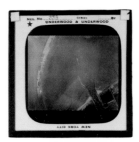

pp. 110 – An aerial photograph showing that the entrance to the canal had been partially blocked.

pp. 114 – The wrecks at low tide.

pp. 122 – Admiral Beatty, commander of the Grand Fleet, in conversation with senior Italian and American naval officers.

pp. 113 – The blockships at high tide.

pp. 117 – War grave containing the remains of 14 British dead burried by the Germans near the St. Donaas church in Zeebrugge.

pp. 123 – Rule Britannia!

al spray now mounted on a section
Zeebrugge Mole was presented to
er Keyes by the City of Bruges in 1918
d returned by his son,
es of Zeebrugge and of Dover.
is memorial on Saint George's Day,
the 80th Anniversary of the famous
Zeebrugge Raid.

Bibliography

Bacon, R., *The Concise Story of the Dover Patrol*, London, 1932

Carpenter, A. , *The Blocking of Zeebrugge*, London, 1922

Deseyne, A. , *De Kust Bezet 1914-1918*, Province of West Flanders, 2007

Kendall, P. , *The Zeebrugge Raid 1918. 'The finest Feat of Arms'*, Spellmount, 2009

Lake, D. , *The Zeebrugge and Ostend Raids 1918*, Barnsley, 2002

Pitt, B. , *Zeebrugge*, New York, 1959

Termote, T. , *Oorlog onder water. Unterseeboots Flottille Flandern 1915-1918*, Davidsfonds, 2014

Wikipedia

144

pp. 134 - 135   *At the foot of the eastern Mole in Ostend stand the remains of the bow of the blockship, HMS Vindictive, sunk in the port of Ostend on 10th May 1918.*

pp. 136 - 137   *Admiraal Keyesplein in Zeebrugge. Fragments of the harbour mole into which the "Vindictive" crashed during the raid on Zeebrugge. The monument was inaugurated on 23rd April 1998, to mark the 80th anniversary of the raid.*

pp. 138 - 139   *British and German military cemetery situated at St. Donaas Church., Zeebrugge. This cemetery is the final resting place of many of those killed in the raid.*

pp. 140 - 141   *Graves of Royal Marines and sailors killed in the Raid on Zeebrugge, in the churchyard of St. Donaas Church.*

pp. 142 - 143   *Set into the wall that surrounds the St. Donaas Church. churchyard, close to the entrance, is a white commemorative stone plaque with a profiled edge. This is the Zeebrugge Memorial. On it are the names of 3 officers and 1 crew member killed in the raid.*

THE RAID ON ZEEBRUGGE
–
23rd of April 1918, as seen through
the eyes of Captain Alfred Carpenter, VC

Carl Decaluwé & Tomas Termote

Published in Great Britain in 2015
by Pen & Sword Military
An imprint of Pen & Sword Books Ltd
47 Church StreetBarnsley, South Yorkshire
S70 2AS

© Roularta Books, Belgium
© Pen&Sword, Great Brittain

ISBN 978 1 47385 431 4
A CIP catalogue record for this book is
available from the British Library

Printed and bound in Belgium
Translation Accolade Language Services.
Design Director: Denis Decaluwé

Cover image:
Detail of the scuttled blockships HMS Intreprid and HMS Iphigenia partially blocking the entrance tot the sea lock.

Pen & Sword Books Ltd incorporates the Imprints of Pen & Sword Aviation, Pen & Sword Family History, Pen & Sword Maritime, Pen & Sword Military, Pen & Sword Discovery, Pen & Sword Politics, Pen & Sword Atlas, Pen & Sword Archaeology, Wharncliffe Local History, Wharncliffe True Crime, Wharncliffe Transport, Pen & Sword Select, Pen & Sword Military Classics, Leo Cooper, The Praetorian Press, Claymore Press, Remember When, Seaforth Publishing and Frontline Publishing

For a complete list of Pen & Sword titles please contact

PEN & SWORD BOOKS LIMITED
47 Church Street, Barnsley, South Yorkshire, S70 2AS, England
E-mail: enquiries@pen-and-sword.co.uk
Website: www.pen-and-sword.co.uk

145